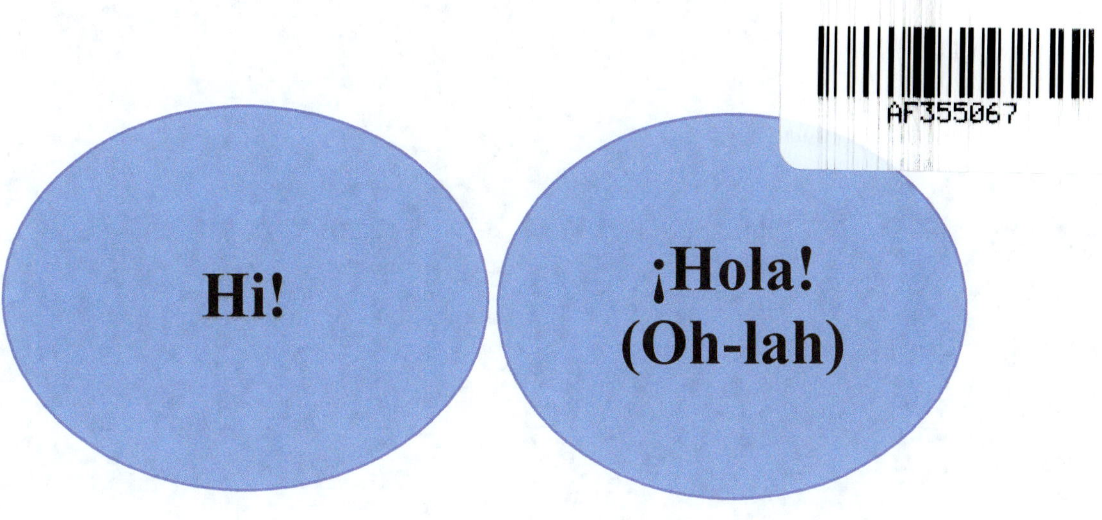

This family photo book belongs to

. . . .

This is my family Esta es mi familia (English-Spanish)

First Edition:2020

ISBN (paperback) 978-93-5426-179-4

Printed in India.

My family

Mi familia (Mee fah-mee-lyah)

STICK PHOTO HERE

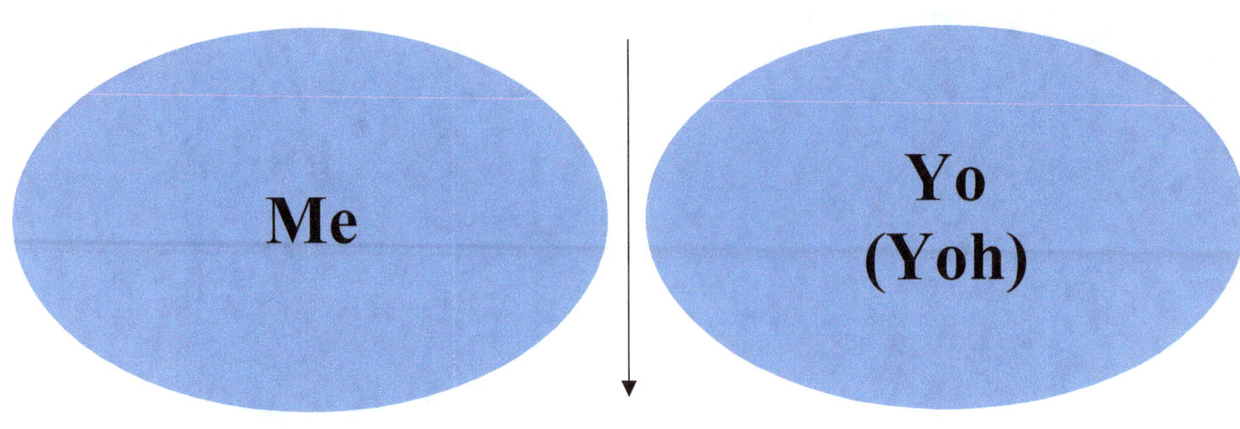

STICK PHOTO HERE

My name is

. . . .

Mi nombre es
(Mee nohm-bray ehs)

. . . .

**My
mother**

**Mi madre
(Mee
mah-dray)**

STICK PHOTO HERE

Her name is

....

Su nombre es
(Soo nohm-bray ehs)

....

My father

**Mi padre
(Mee pah-dray)**

STICK PHOTO HERE

His name is

....

Su nombre es
(Soo nohm-bray ehs)

....

My brother

Mi hermano (Mee ehr-mah-noh)

STICK PHOTO HERE

His name is

....

Su nombre es
(Soo nohm-bray ehs)

....

My sister

Mi hermana (Mee ehr-mah-nah)

STICK PHOTO HERE

Her name is

....

Su nombre es
(Soo nohm-bray ehs)

....

My grandmother

Mi abuela
(Mee
ah-bweh-lah)

STICK PHOTO HERE

Her name is

. . . .

Su nombre es
(Soo nohm-bray ehs)

. . . .

My grandmother

Mi abuela (Mee ah-bweh-lah)

STICK PHOTO HERE

Her name is

....

Su nombre es
(Soo nohm-bray ehs)

....

My
grandfather

Mi abuelo
(Mee
ah-bweh-loh)

STICK PHOTO HERE

His name is

....

Su nombre es
(Soo nohm-bray ehs)

....

My grandfather

Mi abuelo (Mee ah-bweh-loh)

STICK PHOTO HERE

His name is

....

Su nombre es
(Soo nohm-bray ehs)

....

My uncle

**Mi tío
(Mee tee-oh)**

STICK PHOTO HERE

His name is

. . . .

Su nombre es
(Soo nohm-bray ehs)

. . . .

My uncle

**Mi tío
(Mee tee-oh)**

STICK PHOTO HERE

His name is

....

Su nombre es
(Soo nohm-bray ehs)

....

My aunt

**Mi tía
(Mee tee-ah)**

STICK PHOTO HERE

Her name is

. . . .

Su nombre es
(Soo nohm-bray ehs)

. . . .

STICK PHOTO HERE

Her name is

....

Su nombre es
(Soo nohm-bray ehs)

....

**My cousin
(male)**

**Mi primo
(Mee
pree-moh)**

STICK PHOTO HERE

His name is

....

Su nombre es
(Soo nohm-bray ehs)

....

My cousin (female)

Mi prima (Mee pree-mah)

STICK PHOTO HERE

Her name is

....

Su nombre es
(Soo nohm-bray ehs)

....

Also by Anchal Verma

This is my family C'est ma famille: A bilingual English French children's colourful family photo book and beginner book for learning French

My Weekly French Journal: A Year-52-week Goal Tracking Journal for French learners with French proverbs, French tongue twisters, a list of useful French expressions and plenty of other bonus material

French Vocabulary Bank: English-French bilingual vocabulary book of essential French words and phrases

My French Notebook: Ruled 6 sections Notebook/Diary with some useful French expressions

My Language Notebook: Ruled 6 sections Notebook with some useful expressions in different languages

Littérature Fantastique Belge et Belgitude: Étude des nouvelles fantastiques de Jean Ray

For more information about Anchal Verma and her books, visit her website at https://anchalverma.com/